HOUSE OF FACT, HOUSE OF RUIN

Also by Tom Sleigh

POETRY

Station Zed
Army Cats
Space Walk
Bula Matari/Smasher of Rocks
Far Side of the Earth
The Dreamhouse
The Chain
Waking
After One

ESSAYS

The Land between Two Rivers: Writing in an Age of Refugees
Interview with a Ghost

TRANSLATION

Herakles by Euripides

HOUSE OF FACT, HOUSE OF RUIN

POEMS

TOM SLEIGH

Graywolf Press

This publication is made possible, in part, by the voters of Minnesota through a Minnesota State Arts Board Operating Support grant, thanks to a legislative appropriation from the arts and cultural heritage fund, and a grant from the Wells Fargo Foundation. Significant support has also been provided by Target, the McKnight Foundation, the Lannan Foundation, the Amazon Literary Partnership, and other generous contributions from foundations, corporations, and individuals. To these organizations and individuals we offer our heartfelt thanks.

Published by Graywolf Press
250 Third Avenue North, Suite 600
Minneapolis, Minnesota 55401

www.graywolfpress.org

Published in the United States of America

ISBN 978-1-55597-797-9

2 4 6 8 9 7 5 3 1
First Graywolf Printing, 2018

Library of Congress Control Number: 2017938019

Cover design: Kyle G. Hunter

Cover photo: NASA

Contents

HOUSE OF FACT, HOUSE OF RUIN

PART ONE

Three Wishes

Basra, Baghdad, 2016

Down the side of a yellow plastic soap dish, struggling
in soap muck, one of those tiny black ants
that can find a crack in the invisible
flees from the AK of my shadow, and looks
about to spring into the unparted Red Sea
of scum and froth that slimes its feelers
as it rubs and rubs its body
like a tarnished lamp with a genie inside
waiting to stream forth in a cloud of diesel-smoke
from the refineries in Basra
before resolving into a human shape of fire:

could the ant be a sultan bewitched
into the body of an ant? Is that why I hear it say,
Genie, build me a palace!
And in just one night, the genie builds
the Green Zone, it builds what the diplomats
call "the anthill": two Olympic
swimming pools, tennis courts, the D-Fac,
barracks and offices for contractors and Marines,
the gym's row on row of elliptical machines,
my block of prefab trailers behind twenty-foot-high blast walls
and protected by a corrugated steel roof against incoming
so that it's always five p.m. no matter the time of day.

My sultan stares at its bewitched body
like body armor it can't take off reflected
in the shallow sea inside the soap dish.
Above my head, crossing the craters and shell holes
of a ceiling tile, a red ant rubs the lamp of its own body.
First wish: to be the slingstone

muttering to the wound in Goliath's forehead.
Second wish: to trick the invaders into flying away
on the magic carpet of an IED.
Third wish: to make the blast walls vanish
so there's no Green Zone, only a Red Zone.

But now my sultan staggers as if drugged,
moving like a patient moves in a locked psych ward,
some neurotoxin is destroying the genie
inside the sultan's brain, it staggers up the soap dish,
balances woozily on the rim, and then falls into water,
legs and feelers waving weakly until I lift it free
on my finger, wondering if it's going to die, and set it down
on the formica where the sultan lurches and jerks along
and vanishes into the crack between sink and mirror.

First wish: to keep away the Annihilator.
Second wish: to speak the language of the wound.
Third wish: to trick the genie back into the lamp.

1

Lizards

In the desert the lizard is the only liquid flowing under rocks and
  down into crevices, undulating in shadows
like diffusing wisps of smoke that thin to nothingness rippling
  just above the sand dunes.
And just there, in heatwaves turning into air, a mirage begins to
  quiver:

the Desert Fox's Tiger Tanks whose engines make the noises
recorded from the stars, a whine oscillating
underneath the motors' revving, a whine only the lizard can hear.

Artillery fire floating above the clouds of Benghazi, *thum thum
  thunk*
walls dissolving into dust, mosques broadcasting wails of static,
baffled minarets like letters of secret code, a whole codex of holiness
  and banalities.

Is this who we are when we strip off our body armor
which, as we pile it in the rack, looks more vulnerable than our
  nakedness?
I slept in the desert and woke to lizards peering into chicken cages,

the pullets with their heads hidden under wings,
the chicken wire glinting from quartz and mica faintly shining
  upward from the dunes.
The old time killers in their epic understandings had nothing on

what I saw in the still, flat eyes of the lizards: they had that calm,
  jargonizing air of the Sergeant
issuing orders and coordinates of battle: but they themselves, in
  their quivering alertness,
could have been the arrow the scarred killer shoots through

the axe-handles . . . the arrow that comes out
on the far side of time where the island, drifting, swims up through
lightning, then sinks back down into ocean green:

in the deep's primal war room maps unroll themselves,
and there, marked in red, are the circled oil fields, the blow-torch
     refinery flames
looking like souls in illuminated manuscripts, heatwaves

entwining and rippling like two lizards chasing each other over rock,
then freezing in my shadow where the male mounts the female
and they stare, not at each other, but in the same direction, eyes
     expressionless, giving and withholding nothing.

For a Libyan Militia Member

1

Once I cleared the chopper's *wapwapwap*
the airstrip opened up into a treeless drift of sand
where I heard a distant hammer tap against the wind

and smelled scorched concrete wafting from shellholes
in the runway. Then, we were speeding along
in the back of an open truck,

its axles shuddering over hardpan as I rubbernecked
at burned-out tanks, turrets blown to the roadside
seeming somehow sadder than the men who died.

2

Just a boy who played soccer until the revolution,
he learned, with a bad shoulder, to fire an AK-47,
shoot off a mortar so he didn't burn his hands, talk away fear—

the radio broadcasting endless hero/victim chatter
sent him racing behind a wall, hiding from the sniper's crosshairs—
pinwheeling shrapnel sent him to the hospital—

where he suffered as much from boredom as his wound.
Playing with a lizard he holds by the tail,
the panting ribs pulse as he dangles it

head down, his bandaged cheek, crisscrossed with tape, looking
like it aches. The hot breeze dries sweat
from his face as the lizard whiplashes loose, scrambling

across the sheet to disappear under the bed,
one wounded foot leaving pinpricks of blood—
not a trail or code, just the tail left dangling

in the boy's fingers as he laughs and, swinging
it around, shows it to his mother frowning,
What's that? and snatches it away.

3

Each time the boy, grown-up now, is forced to flash
ID, his scar tissue's calligraphy writes on his body
the history of his own scalloped, twisted flesh
shrugging off my pose of objectivity:

shrinking, puckering, the skin grafts on
his burns shine white as phosphorus in the sun:
and whatever I write down, the counter-text
scrawled on his cheek revises itself each time his mouth flexes

into a grin or frown, as year by year whatever's
written there gets that much harder to decipher,
that much further from the war, until in the mirror
he'll see and won't see his own scars.

4

In shade and sunlight the lizard grows a new tail
that writes in dust over a broken cobble
its slithering trail until it stops short, heart pulsing in its throat,
red eyes fixed on that foreign shape which takes out

a notebook, scribbles *green and brown skin, broken black diamonds*
arranged in vertical stripes, claws that look like hands
of a fever victim. And then scribbled notes
in neutral tones about mortar fire, flak jackets,

the strap on the helmet that's always too loose or too tight,
the boy's bombed house, shockwaves blowing out
the windows to let in riot gas, an adrenaline rush,
the smell of tears chemical as ammonia, and as harsh.

5

All around me the sound of men sleeping,
their bodies shifting slightly in their dreaming,
the engines of the trucks still cooling
giving off little ticks and pings.

And then I was climbing out of my blankets to slip under
the tent's canopy, stumbling away from mumbling and snores,
the desert cold making the dew-damped sand stiffen
so it crunched underfoot as I crept beyond the watchman

to take a piss: and at the edge of the camp, near the chickens
in their coop, heads tucked under wings,
was a fox staring back, or what I thought was a fox
ducking down into the shadows and disappearing behind the trucks

that in the morning would obliterate
its precise, four-clawed tracks that the next night
and the next would keep on coming back, until the chickens got
eaten, or the fox was killed. Then pattering of my own piss brought

me back into the cold, the sky overhead dark and bright,
bundled bodies in the dawn beginning to levitate—
whose elbows dreamed up the chokehold? Who pushes
back the boundaries so that no-man's-land is

the only *heimat*, homeland, *patrie*? Who strips us
of our shadows so that our histories turn to glass?
And then it was time for breakfast, to sip tea, smoke,
and take my place beside the others in the truck.

List

Gunfire night and day in the old city won't let up
as the aura of exhaustion floats me beyond sleep

and the planet on its axis tilts back a degree
until the world, off-kilter, spins loose from gravity.

I'm back crossing desert hard pan, the militia commander
napping in the front seat, the sun hazed out so you can't tell sky

from pebbled waste. The blasted tanks perspire
in mist burning off, their turrets and barrels blistered.

Fairouz is singing about her broken heart, how her star,
like her lover, doesn't whisper to her anymore.

In some adjutant's drawer, the Brother Leader's
list of who will be terminated, imprisoned, tortured

goes on and on, name after name that ceases to exist
the moment the sentence has been passed.

But Ashur, Mohammed, Ali come back to life
as I scribble down their names and the wind begins to cuff

the landrover jouncing until our joints ache
and the dead men staring back from between these letters,

faces lit up for a moment as they share a smoke,
turn away from me, shrugging their shoulders

as if to say, *Who cares?* as the landrover, shifting gears,
disappears into the dust kicked up by its own tires.

Dream

Scrounging, hammering scrap into pots and pans,
sewing whatever rags the guards allowed in,
you fault your own steps in the sun falling
slant on walls cratered by an RPG.
                                            But when
those bars at last spring open, you're always late,
your train is pulling out, suitcase gone,
clothes turned back to rags, running barefoot,
the television floating far out on the ocean
replaying your execution on and on.
You wait for the hand to reach inside the dream,
your mother's voice to say,
                                        This dream is done.
And all you know of freedom is how small you feel
returning to your cell when you lift your arms
for the pat down and smell her smell.

Litany

It isn't camels and sheep and an underground house
or an abandoned oasis, the shaded grass littered with fallen dates.

It isn't tankers lined up on the horizon,
or sand dunes asking nothing and giving nothing as they creep.

It isn't the sculpture of a golden fist crushing a fighter jet,
or graffiti shouting *Death or Freedom*.

It's the way vodka in the house of the imam
can be hidden in a plastic water bottle.

It's Ashur's unpublished papers on prostrate cancer,
the patient with the catheter released from the hospital

for just one night who goes home to his wife
and they figure out a way to make love.

It's what the German doctor whose name means "joy"
meant by the psychopathology of nations.

It's the joke about bullets being fired off into the air
because the air makes such a good target not even a blind man
    can miss.

It's not the houses burned, the young men shot or kidnapped,
it's not the anti-aircraft guns positioned where your house was.

It's what no one will say about what no one else will say.
It's what anyone who knows what they shouldn't say knows.

It's what the Revolution whispers about one war everywhere
in the ear of a drone watching a camel

rippling through heatwaves on a screen.

A Drone in the Promised Land

Quneitra, Syria: Golan Heights

I was streaming my way through things, a signal
registering clouds of noise, when I lost
myself, a drone gone out of range, and fell
into this second life where what is past
keeps on reoccurring: so in that ruin
of a church where propaganda said Jesus
preached here on his way to his crucifixion
and where graffiti in fading spray paint shouts
to the abandoned town, *May fever make
our enemies sweat,* sharing the doubts
of Thomas I felt the wall's powdery
shell holes as if I too were fingering Christ's
wounds—thumb-sized for AK,
fist-sized for 20, two fists for 50.

David and Goliath. My opposites
and twins. David whirls his slingstone, Goliath
sways top-heavy in his armor. The diplomats
in secret talks shuttle back and forth,
but the slingstone, once set whirling, won't
wait to find its target: behind my detachment,
I thought one side would run, the other stand its ground—
but the seismic spasm of the wound
in Goliath's forehead pleaded its own cause:
the blood running down into the giant's eyes
blinded the young victor to trajectories
the stone would plot on its own, regardless
of the experts and commentators' noise
above the armor clattering down in the replays.

———————

All standing-off ended when the stone opened
its viral, spreading gash of a mind-wound:
ours became theirs, the big picture went blurry
though the details were never sharper, ally
turned enemy, then morphed into data,
our trust in our protectors jagged and spiked
like an epileptic's brainwaves, jet trails stacked
in the blue as the hydra-headed sky camera
made no distinctions between winners and losers.
And ever since, I can't help but see that town
stripped of doors, windows, shutters right down
to the knobs, hinges, screws, all of it piled in
trucks for auction back home and neither
David or Goliath will be the highest bidder.

———————

On the fuselage, is the painted-on muzzle
of a wolf meant to give its shadow, streaking across
the villages, what the old man whose house was
blown up, told me? "A way to make us feel
the blow. . . ." Is it meant to conjure up a being
from the ash-pit of Jehoshaphat,
its heat-seeking, infrared teeth gnashing
at a keystroke that will incinerate
whatever scruple holds it back? I wanted
to feel my observer's stance was both accountable
and enviable in its lack of malice, wanted
to think I stood on a different scruple
of legitimate detachment—but the camera
kept watch from a locked room in Nevada.

———————

My circuitry most fallible when I feel
the Power leading me to Canaan, my night vision
lashless, unblinking as a Sphinx or squirrel,
I watched nail-holes being punched into that town
by neutrinos invisibly crucifying the oleanders
as I loped across the skies in my remote control
stealth, a joystick guiding me at will.
And yet the growling *thunk* of a tank's gears
downshifting through the abandoned gardens,
the radar installations' digitally
flashing tongues spreading like migraines
above the fraying jet trails, couldn't deny
the shattered cistern trickling rain water
and birdsong swooping through the hospital corridor.

———————————

My dream's wolfishness had gone undercover,
the penis sheathed, the muzzle shrinking to
the perfectly proportioned nose of a statue
that a stray bullet shaved, but didn't shatter.
And in an old family Bible, the onion skin
scored with births penciled in in a fading,
Palmer Method hand, while deaths scrawled in pen
.sprawl across the page, I see the runny ink spidering
down to where the last name marks the end
of a generation. And up through that name,
its water-slicked roundness shining in the stream
that divides the oaks of Elah from no-man's-land,
the chosen stone, dreaming its own dream,
turns over and over in David's hand.

Propaganda

Her tolerant smile says back to my smile, Of course I'm used to
　　this, it's just what someone
like you would ask, nor was she wrong in her assessment—
but aloud she said, Yes, certainly that kind of question would have
　　to be addressed
if one really wanted a cultural exchange with the West:
but you have to take in certain Islamist attitudes and how the fate
　　of women
must be bettered, and minorities too, not by slapping each other
　　in the face
but by the gradual homogenization of attitudes—which takes time—
after all, she says, I did my dissertation on Shelley and the Chartists,
and I can tell you that liberal attitudes such as you have are easy
　　to hold
when the argument's written—but here, where the argument
keeps coming up against the Koran where what is written is written
　　for all time
there's not much room for legal maneuvering that wouldn't result
　　in brutal repercussions: and so we go slow here
and the police go easy too, so really, we have our freedoms if at
　　times on the sly,
and as my gay friends from London tell me, Damascus is paradise,
　　even if under the gay-dar . . .
and here, she said, is a video disk that will show what the Israelis
　　did in Lebanon:
Savage Israeli Savage Beast read the 18-point type: and in the
　　photos,
a dead child looking stagey in a man's arms, his eyes gone unfocused
　　in that way
people crying have when they stare into a camera, but weirdly direct
　　when the viewer pulls back,
accusing, denouncing, *What do you know about atrocity?*

the scream of the frozen open mouth showing gold fillings in the
    molars.
Just a crude photo-op, the way one website claimed, the dead child
nothing but a fever victim offered up to the camera's eye?
A donkey in the background pissing down its leg,
a man in the foreground carrying a dead child with his head turned
    to the side
as if he were Christ as a homunculus being taken off the cross,
but really just a boy blown up by a bomb, his forehead ungashed,
his body limp but not looking injured, until you saw how his arm
    dangled
at an impossible angle: as if he'd been playing softball and, winding
    up to pitch,
his arm had gotten stuck in the furthest reach of his stiff-armed
    swing backwards,
the shoulder twisted under his t-shirt into a ridge of spasmed
    muscles
gone completely dead: all right, here's the boy's picture, and here
    she is on Facebook,
black neck-length hair curled but without fuss, the gray touched up,
her blouse a tasteful striped gray and white befitting the Minister
    of Expatriates.
And here she is in an email from a journalist pal, *Isn't she that
    charming little monster we met?*
And yes, the State Department's frozen her assets and isolated her
    as a main supporter of a criminal regime, and no American
may ever have dealings with her again: and when I look at the
    photo closer, the whole body
of the donkey seems to be giving in to taking that piss among
    crazily stacked blocks of rubble, cratered shell holes,
and a man's shoe walking all on its own out of the frame.

The Advance

1

Out the barred window sand bags
in a sagging wall surround the guard post
where a soldier half-hidden by the flag
holds his rifle on his knees and looks a little lost.

It's Sunday and quiet, the traffic noise
off aways, the sea behind the post flat as the tarps
pulled tight over the troop trucks.
Somewhere down the hall soldiers are being boys,

telling some joke in Arabic
in which I'm pretty sure I hear the word "zubrak":
I walk between shelves loaded with canned rations,

the cool expiring slowly in the high-ceilinged room
while a pinned-up PSYOPS leaflet declares,
If you sleep in a cemetery, you're bound to have nightmares.

2

No one sees the doll's decapitated head small
and neat in rubble. Never tired or sleepy,
the head is its own country
obstinately surviving, the pupil

of its one eye peering through the glass's pure
transparency. And a few feet away lie its slim, plastic,
long-legged thighs almost like
an obscenity the eye watches over—

no one in the street, nothing but bolt-marks
from tank-treads scarring the concrete
to give any of it drama—and what

about the way the lips' frozen smirk
keeps daring me to touch the sexless V
between the thighs staring up at me?

3

The barracks dissolve into a reef of rubble in the fog.
On either side of the road, crater after crater
flashes with glints of glass, plastic bags,
a chair leg clinging to a dismembered chair.

The TV station, the power stacks
thrusting up through mist, the black-bearded posters
and banners strung across
the streets lead to an absolute nowhere:

all that's left in the emptied town
after the army pulled out are PSYOPS leaflets
fluttering up around the car that winds

down the coast road deeper into mist, headlights
probing like instruments in a wound
they illuminate the more they violate.

2

Lady Justice

What the camera sees today is a prisoner
on his knees as sun puts on an orange jumpsuit
to light up the sand dune waste

where the man's executioner poses beside him
for a selfie. The prisoner is talking
the self-incriminating confession

his murderer has scripted for him to say.
Against the light you can see him squint
to read the large-sized print scrawled

on cue cards, his unshaven face floating
in the heat as his Adam's apple moves up and down.
The world is everything that is the case, said Wittgenstein,

but today you'd have to say he's wrong:
to use such a little knife to cut off a man's head—
even to think of this makes Lady Justice glad

she's got her blindfold on, so she doesn't
have to see what she can't not see
going on inside her head of what they did.

Enhanced Interrogation Techniques

1

Everything that's happening isn't me
doing it, it's what the cold's doing, the music's
doing, it's what gravity's doing to the guy
and if I can't imagine what it's like
how much less can someone
outside the whole situation see it straight on
when what somebody else is doing
might be worse than what I'm doing,
and say there's only concertina wire
between you and the town and you're
getting mortared all the time, and if infantry brings
you a guy you think is shooting mortars, scaring
him with a muzzled dog doesn't seem like the worst trick.
I was willing to try it. I didn't know it wasn't going to work.

2

So let's say the source is in a field in a tent
at dawn when the desert breeze
has dried the dew and all the ropes relent
so that he gently sways at ease
from its supporting steel pole
that as far as orders go is in accord
with how far we've been told we can go
but if you find yourself speaking on the record,
strictly speaking we're bound
by the memo which says that using a knot
like this so the guy can't make a sound
when the rope goes even slightly taut,
might be pushing it, so we need to be aware
of how all this might look to the press corp.

3

I was dreaming about S-2, just like my uncle in the War
—S-2 means Intelligence. I was taking two prisoners
back to the rear but my dream kept putting this Major
in my way—we got stopped by the Major who asked where
we were headed and when I said, "The rear,"
the Major said, pointing toward the front, "The rear
is back there. Don't you know any better?"
And so I said, "Yes, Sir!" and turned the prisoners
around until the Major walked out of sight.
And then we turned around again and one prisoner shook
his head and said in some dream tongue that
I completely got, "Your officers are
just as dumb as ours." And we all stood there
laughing, and all of us were thinking, *Just our luck!*

4

As if all this is being scanned by the green light
in the barcode scanner, I'm walking around in aisle 8
looking for Ding Dongs when the florescence makes me
think of forcing guys to do the frog squat or how we'd
strip a guy and make him sit in the snow naked or maybe we'd
put a sandbag over a guy's head so that this one guy
keeps begging me to take off his hood just so he
can see the sun and walk around a little while the green light
keeps flashing, and the total keeps increasing as I get
closer to the head of the line so that I'm thinking what a mess
this guy is, how isolation is just flattening him, and so I
go and do the only thing I can do—interrogate him about
his abuse—and the machine in its machine voice says,
Please place the items in your bag and take your receipt.

5

Part of what I did was turn myself into a dog.
I mean think like a dog. We had dog handlers
and they'd cue the dog to lunge and bark at the prisoner
who'd be wearing blacked-out goggles so he couldn't see the muzzle
on the dog, he just knew there was this dog
going nuts in the room with him, a big angry dog
that might scare him so much he'd piss his pants,
literally. But then he'd figure out the dog
wasn't going to attack. By this time I'd be sick
of the whole thing but then I'd have to turn into gravel
or concrete or plywood because we'd make
him crawl across gravel, concrete, plywood, we'd have three strobes
going at once, we'd lock this guy in a little box
and like me he's afraid of insects and I'd have to turn into ants.

6

In one side of my brain I'm seeing him healthy and in the other
I'm standing guard at three in the morning
outside the shipping container where he's
inside with super loud music and flashing lights, and these
four sergeants are standing around me, all wanting
to get in on the interrogation and I'm a specialist, and they're
like, *Let's go and fuck the guy up*, and I have to control these guys
who outrank and outnumber me, and they've got weapons
and I don't because I'm guarding the prisoner—and then his face
is on these two screens again and in one he's just totally broken
down while in the other he's got this perfect moustache
that somehow doesn't seem to belong to his face and guys
are banging on the shipping container or throwing stones
at it and I'm yelling at the guy, *How do I control this situation?*

7

You might think this is not a good defense either,
but the things I did weren't really that horrible.
I mean, I saw some really horrible torture.
And I'm sure like every torturer would say this,
"Other people are doing worse things, other people
are carrying things much further than this—"
like the guys we were leaving out in the cold,
I was always the guy who went out and kept checking
on them, but most of our people just sat in the office watching
DVDs while these guys were out there, out in the cold.
I was bringing them in and warming them up.
I never hit a prisoner, or shocked them, did mock executions.
But sure, hypothermia or stress positions
might do more damage than beating someone up . . .

8

But there are other answers, too. You're in a war zone
and things get blurred. We wanted intelligence but it really
became absolutely morally impossible for me
to continue when I realized that most of the people we
were dealing with were innocent. But it was a very blurry line—
I can say I was following orders and that's partly true.
I was wondering, *At what time do I put my foot down?*
And there were times when I said, *I'm not crossing this line.*
I saw barbaric traits begin to seep out of me—you're
faced with two choices—disobey direct orders or
become a monster. It made it easier if I thought
I was actually dealing with a real-life bad guy—but
as I said, these are flawed arguments, but if you
think of it that way, it makes it easier to do.

Where the Magic Ends

1

Only in words is she more than a slave-woman,
only in words does she boil the forty thieves

in jars of oil, only in words does she gain
her freedom by killing her master's enemies

one by one. And only in words can she
triumph in her tale when bulldozers

roll in to work their magic in the townships,
the woodcutter shouting "Open sesame!"

to the cave door while all around him piles up
rebar, mortar, brick. And when that magic's

almost done, that's the moment when the sultan
lies back, entranced by the voice that spins

the tale that lets the poor man wallow in the shine
of jewels, murder the sultan, marry his daughter,

and heft in his own mind the scimitar
that dangles by its syllables above his neck.

2

The IED jammer in the SUV sent up a loud whine
we had to talk over, while the guys with guns

up in the front seat scanned right and left at each corner.
Stalled in heatwaves bouncing off the cars,

we kept our eyes to ourselves, learning the conqueror's
subtle self-subjugation, spent and obedient before

our shrugging off the war, pretending that our words
weren't the only ones that would be heard.

But where the booksellers killed in Al-Mutanabbi Street
once leaned out from their stalls, or would float

on the magic carpets of the pages of a book,
reading, reading late into the night, it's said

that the day the city was invaded the river ran red,
but on the next day the water ran black with ink.

My Tiger

He tells me take out my keys, please, and do I
      have any other metal
on me? In me? The MRI works by magnetism
so you don't want a pin in your hip flying loose!
I lie down in the metal cocoon and he pulls
tight the straps. He's sending me toward the donut hole
where I'll pass into magnetic fields a thousand times
stronger than the earth's, a field that if I
could see it would look like a helmet fitting down low
over my eyes, almost blinding me—
not like the kind Roland wore, but like the guys
in the armored vehicle I was in a few months ago.

He tells me this will take a while: would I prefer
      a sedative . . . ?
then he leaves the room and the jackhammering
of the machine fills the voids in my skull.
Immobile on the table, I feel like that stuffed
tiger nailed tail-first to the wall of an artist pal,
my head dangling down resting on a stool.
Jimi Hendrix's "Machine Gun" "tearing
me all apart" echoes in the armored vehicle again.
Why don't soldiers in the field play Bach?
If you're a tiger, though, maybe you like Hendrix
more, maybe Hendrix "shooting me down"

gets closer to the condition of sweating
      in your flak jacket
while some NGO geek yammers on and on about
food aid not getting through? The tiger sits there licking

its paws while a man on TV shows off his scars
that look like claws could have made them as he
tells the TV about the secret torture chamber
people drive right by every day to work the way
he used to, sipping heavily sugared tea.
I'm going up in an elevator, watching
it all come down when a grenade sails through
the air and explodes right in front of me.

Oh tiger, I know you disdain to look at me, me
      a goof of a tiger,
my poor splayed paws, my tongue balled up
between my fangs as if I'd reached some absolute
limit at the edge of growls tranqued up
to keep me docile—though only a real tiger
would try to jump over the concrete moat and scale
the bullet-proof, plexi-glass wall. My pupils
narrowed down to slits watch it all come back
when my helmet slides over my eyes and blocks the view
of what the male and female soldier intend to do:
smooth barrels of their AKs press into my back

and against my chest, her small breasts and his
      big gut multiplying
all around me in the security mirror's
promiscuous angles in a caress
they never meant that was almost tender . . .
the nightingale retreats before me
vale by vale and sees, as it flies over the pass,
the battle concluding with a man blowing
a horn until his brain breaks and comes oozing
out his ears. Oh, the knights and horses all lie slain,
their lemans sitting grieving beside them,
my tiger padding his silent way from the groin

up into the brain. Their wounds are gashes,
          not clean-torn holes
a .20 caliber machine gun makes. Do I
wake or sleep while the voids inside my brain
get mapped in the differences between
the earth's magnetic field and the machine's?
And what are my brainwaves doing to their corpses
being stripped as they lie sprawled in clear
mountain air, looking more post-coital
than post battle, like models hired for the day?
And see how my tiger turns his head away,
made shy by the face of so much bliss.

Kibera

I made, as usual, the usual mistake:
I was asking about the heart rather than the eye:
a picture of Jesus's heart tacked high on one wall
of the tiny shack among a million tiny shacks,
the heart one of the 3D kind that if you look at it
from one angle glows with holy light but if you cock
your head just so sheds big bloody tear-shaped drops.
That's when the young man who lived there, my guide,
took me to see the orphans who sang a rehearsed song
that wavered in the ear, faces remote, hard to read,
ribs slatted through skin as if the body was a blind
keeping light from pouring in.
                              Meanwhile, the heart, undaunted,
kept imposing itself—wanted to call them "a fearful stain"
who "can't go home again." But looking through the eye,
you see it differently.
                        And then I thought, How differently?
The way a fly sees, multiplying one roof furrow
into a vast mosaic jittering that is itself
a kind of wonder, a pulsing surge of roof glitter
the heart falls down before, not knowing what to say?
Or the way a mosquito's many lenses
see overlapping images, hands, arms, faces
in a kind of tantric whirl?
                            Or like eyespots
of algae, called stigma, the same as Jesus's
wounds, that float in the polluted stream smelling
of goat and human shit, and that propel themselves
toward regions of more concentrated light
so as to work in microscopic factories to
manufacture oxygen that even the highest
of highrises must breathe?
                           The kids I was giving

suckers to weren't smiling or reacting—
                                    they stood there
staring, just as I was staring, their wary human stares
before singing all together, as the orphanage women
cued them, *Hello, dear visitor, welcome, how are you?*

And maybe that's all that I could see—just their impersonal
alertness when they stuck the suckers in their mouths,
sucking for the calories as much as the sweetness
my guide said.

                    But day or night, if you could look through
the eyes without the heart, you'd see the eye cure
itself of blindness by the discharge of fluid from itself;
you'd see the blind regaining sight after being blind
for twenty years;
                    you'd see some who are born blind
without any visible defect in the eye.
                                    And if you were dying
in your hut or up in your highrise, and you could silence
the heart, the right thing to do would be for someone
to close your eyes as you died and open them again
on your funeral pyre since it isn't right that any
human being should see the eyes at the moment
of dying or that the eyes not be open to the flames.

3

What Is

There's a painting in which Christ is tied to a marble pillar,

while three men stand aside, paying no attention to the little,
two-tailed whip, no longer than the whipper's forearm,

raised to strike. And there's another painting of a battle

in which men killing and men dying stare into each other's eyes
not in hatred or enmity but immense resignation, as if saying,

This is what is and I know it can't be otherwise. The only one

showing emotion is a horse baring its teeth, the splayed hairs
of its long tail flecked ornately with spots of blood.

And there's a painting of a woman who's supposed to be a whore,

her wet hair on her shoulders painted strand by strand,
her shoulders and neck big and sturdy.

The pictures are so silent in their silent spaces,

the worlds long past, the people painted seeming fated
to be graced or disgraced in those final postures,

the wall ungiving to any other motive than the painter's,

their bloody and carnal selves traded for an image,
pain flattened into paint for whatever the going rate is,

like the guys doing day labor at the U-Haul place on the corner,

hanging around all day, waiting to go somewhere so they
don't have to go back broke to wherever they sleep at night.

The *ranchera* blasting on my neighbor's radio sings

far away there's a grand ranch, far away where I used to live, yahaha!
and the music's tinny blare that won't relent

brings to mind another painting of an immense iceberg dwarfing

a tiny ship frozen in the floe, the blue light
emanating down into the depths of the slob ice pulsing,

keeping time for the hearts frozen beneath the paint.

Negatives

*"The trick is, I find, to tone your wants and tastes low down enough,
and make much of negatives, and of mere daylight and the skies."*
—WALT WHITMAN, FROM *NOTES OF A HALF-PARALYTIC*

1

Low tide midnight. The sulfur smelling bay.
The little green island disappearing twice a day.

And me practicing with Whitman a raw
form of brinksmanship, lisping to myself *the low*

and delicious word death, and again, death death death . . .
Despite the butterfly glued to his finger in the staged photograph,

by writing the dying soldiers' last letters, by keeping vigil,
did Whitman learn what was fake, what real?

And when he writes that the real war will never get
in the books, is what drowns out the standard elegiac

the *heavy-pouring constant rain* of the *unending,
universal mourning-wail of women, parents, orphans?*

Or is what really filters and fibers our blood
not more words, but just more blood?

2

The real war appears only in the soldiers'
strength and animality and lawless gait

among the hundreds of unnamed, unseen lights
and shades of the battlefields North and South

that are nothing but a vast, central hospital:
"He seem'd quite willing to die—he had become

very weak and had suffer'd a good deal,
and was perfectly resign'd, poor boy. What I saw of him

here, under the most trying circumstances,
with a painful wound, and among strangers,

I can say that he behaved so brave, so composed,
and sweet and affectionate, it could not be surpass'd.

Such things are gloomy—the meaning of which,
after due time, appears to the soul."

3

The inmates didn't so much look for you under their bootsoles as
trample you under their regulation shoes from *maquiladoras*.

They scorned the paper butterfly glued to your finger
but they called you cool for sitting with dying soldiers.

They got, but also mocked, your need to kiss dying soldiers.
"Doesn't this guy know that in a hospital the reason for flowers

is to cover up the smell?" One said that your prophecies
about democracy turned to sour grapes at being ignored.

And Maurice, a lifer, who got an A on his paper *How I Became a
    Murderer*,
said, "Whitman's the kind of guy who when he first gets to the cage

thinks everybody's out to kill him, but learns little by little
that not everybody is—which is maybe why he sounds so hopeful

at first . . . but what does that matter if after ten years
your thoughts don't have the energy to climb the wall?"

4

Doldrums. Damp heat. The Walt Whitman Mall's
air-conditioned spaces, infrared beams of scanners

tallying up the costs, the digital tidal
overflow reflected in the long coattails

of his bronze duster. His paralysis at the end
is our paralysis now, all done with blab and bluster,

his tongue hobbled, himself his own memorial.
But see the tide flowing back over the island

so that everywhere you look the weeds are all give
and go, slack and taut, while out to sea vast slicks of sun

shiver like the fevered flesh of men
he sits beside, talking, musing, wafting a fan,

learning what it means in death to live
by learning what to make of negatives.

The Drowned and the Saved

If all of us were to try to kill ourselves at least once, then all of us would know nothing more than that: which is why Primo Levi may have had a dizzy spell before he fell over the stair railing to his death, which would mean that he didn't commit suicide but instead felt light-headed and lost his balance. He was a small man, five foot five, only about one hundred twenty pounds, and if you think of the disproportionate weight of his head in relation to the rest of his body, then it makes sense that he landed more or less on his skull. And so Auschwitz may not have been his nemesis so much as his exhaustion and depression and the medication he was taking after a prostate operation.

But as he plunges down the stairwell, Auschwitz is the easiest explanation: for some, it confirms their heroic/tragic notions of what a concentration camp must be, of how the barbwire and *Arbeit Macht Frei* and the SS joke about coming in by Gate A and going out through the crematorium at Station Zed become like the two pillars that were said to mark the limits of the known world beyond which lay Atlantis. Which of course was destroyed by the gods and buried by an earthquake that reared up a huge wave that swept Atlantis away. But Levi has just received his mail from the concièrge—a few newspapers, some advertising leaflets—nothing that might noticeably have upset him, nothing that could have built itself into the ship that would have carried him out onto the open sea where he could witness Ulysses, Dante's version of him, anyway, sailing through those pillars toward Mount Purgatory where a vast whirlpool drags him and his entire crew down.

For Levi, there was another whirlpool whirling in his own apartment that has nothing to do with the drowned or the saved, but with what a friend once called "the hateful strength of the dying": his mother and mother-in-law, both living with him, both in their nineties, cared for by the same nurse. It's said by a rabbi who claimed to have received a phone call from Levi just minutes before he killed himself, that Levi told him he could no longer stand looking at the senile, ailing women, because they reminded him of the men dying stretched on the benches at Auschwitz. If you imagine these old women in a tiny boat spinning round and round inside their own brains, and Levi watching them spin, unable to help them back onto dry land . . . then? Then what?

Maybe what's more useful is to think of his purported suicide as an inevitable requirement, a wound that never heals, a reason for others to imagine that the events that led to Auschwitz can never be escaped because it confirms in some obscure way that life matters—that one died not because one got dizzy and fell by accident over a balcony railing which at most came up to Levi's navel, but because even forty years later Levi was still in the lager, waiting for the word he feared, but knew was coming: *Wstawàch!* Get up! Unlike one other famous Holocaust surviving suicide, Jean Améry, who Levi once said was a "theoretician of suicide," Levi was concerned with chemical reactions. His last unfinished novel purports to be the correspondence between a man and a young woman, in which the man reveals to her the chemistry that allows one to make omelets and fancy sauces. Béchamel, for example, combines butter and flour, and milk. Maybe he was thinking of butter combining with flour when he fell. Or maybe he was thinking of how silver in the mountain can be enriched when other materials enter it and form chemical concentrations that raise the yield. Or maybe he wasn't thinking at all; maybe thinking or the kinds of thoughts he was having are beside the point, not because they don't matter, but because we won't ever know them, confused or clear, anguished or distracted—and so what we're left with are guesswork and uncertainties against the lager's barracks and barbed-wire fences . . . and, of course, the forensics: age, weight, height, sex, a precise description of what a fall from four flights up would do to a human brain.

In the background of his death, in black and white, footage of the Holocaust plays over and over on computer screens and movie screens, commentators in magazines speak of his books as prolonged, if delayed, suicide notes; they say that the nature of hell is its inescapability, that he died still in Auschwitz forty years later.

But still—what if he *did* have a dizzy spell? And what if he was thinking about Béchamel, or how heat causes the egg's globe-shaped proteins to move around more and more violently, so that the collisions between the strands of protein weaken the bonds between them so that the different strands can bond together— which is why egg whites go from transparent to opaque as they are cooked.

The boat sinks. The eggs get eaten. The body falls.

And if that's all that we have to think about, and if suffering is inside us and outside us, and if an egg has at least chemical awareness of the heat that is denaturing it, making it into another kind of being, then the newspapers and advertising leaflets, the plunge through the airshaft to the floor below, all the circumstances that lead Levi to climb the rail or to simply lose his balance, are whirling around us now, and who can tell if it's more terrifying to be sucked down, or to have been sucked down and now, still alive, emerge back up riding the rim of a bubble expanding as it rises from the bottom of the sea?

Down from the Mount

i.m. Le Bataclan

> *The Angel of History . . . is turned towards the past. Where we see the appearance of a chain of events, he sees one single catastrophe, which unceasingly piles rubble on top of rubble and hurls it before his feet.* —WALTER BENJAMIN

And so we come back into our own, down from the mount
where there are no tablets, no burning bush,
no prophet's *I'm-the-end-all-be-all* rant,

no mouth-terrorists twisting words, no witnesses
insisting they're more sinned against than sinning.
No hands without blood, no hand wringing—

just the hazed-out headlights of a cab,
the canal running past rust-fretted terraces
and warehouses. Just the sunned on drab

of raincoats sauntering through mayflies
coptering off the river. Just cellphone voices,
raggedy-ass gunfire—and then, under the TV's

muted stillness, the planet's bagpipe under-drone
on just another day of coming storm.

Our Angel's back is to the future,
the winds of time blow open
his wings as he watches eon after eon
pile up its wreckage: salamanders,

the golden frogs
of Panama, giant slime,
the tuneless hum
of dead nations' flags,

decommissioned bombs,
all our dead ones like after-party
stragglers who

keep showing up in dreams,
saying, *I want you*
to keep this for me.

The dogs are terrorists to cats, the cats
terrorists to rats, the rats terrorists
to each other watching each others'
terror. The rock band warming up is shut

inside its wall of noise. The rain's footage
runs backward into drains,
the public statues seem to suffocate from rage,
the President of the republic of pigeons

flies in circles with his entourage,
the wire-woven wreaths in the cemeteries
come loose one petal at a time. A fountain

spouting from a monster's mouth runs dry
as flying beyond the future we couldn't own,
sky-eyes-and-ears keep recording in the sun.

No underworld to go down to, no courageous
cricket to leap down to it and bring their images
back—no way to make their wounds seal up, no way
to call them back into their bodies'

negating shells—no alarmed wings whirring,
no words of what they know down there
about up here, only this endless TV chirping
about what happened as they tried to hide or lay there

on the dance floor, unmoving. But in another time, outside
the city wall, as two friends talk about love and the soul,
they hear the crickets who once were human beings lull

the countryside to sleep and tell how that singing
was a pleasure so divine for the ones chorusing
that they forgot to eat or drink—and so they died.

———————————

from the *Odyssey, Bk. XXIV*

As bats that come awake in a cave made
eerie by their rustling, when first one
then another, all clinging to the stone
and to each other in a cluster, spread
their wings and begin to flit and gibber,

so the slaughtered were led by Hermes holding
his fateful, golden wand, all flittering
beyond the Ocean past the Gates of the Sun,
past that place where undreamed dreams are born,
to these open fields and meadows: and here

other phantoms gather to ask them who
caused their wounds that still bleed
up there, even as the god leads
the way into the silence they fly through.

All the Ways Dust Tastes

I tried to write about your death using
a slo-mo evocation of going snorkeling
in the Adriatic, the two of us diving

underwater to an ancient Roman wall
submerged by an earthquake, the silted mortar
growing seaweed swirling all around us

as we dove deeper toward the ooze
where I thought I saw the chipped and grooved
handle of an amphora, the fired clay

still not shattered by the tide. And as I
dive into a crevice where the wall washed
away, and stretch out my hand to shove

my fingers into murky silt, I feel
a sea urchin's spine's sharp prick—a small wound,
barely noticeable, that festers, swells,

and six months later, the splinter still lodged
in my finger, bursts—which was when you sighed,
Aleš, a little too loudly, the way you always do

when thinking how to frame bad news:
"I must admit that I'm not convinced by
this version of me that you've rigged up—

it all seems like a lot of props: the Roman wall,
the swirling seaweed . . . and if I remember right,
weren't these lines lifted from another poem

you wrote? Something about a hospital
in Berlin and you walking down a corridor
with your rear end hanging out of your gown

(a 'johnny,' no?) and staggering down the ward
clutching your IV pole? Forgive me for asking:
but just how well did you know this so-called *Aleš*?

Just because I died in a stupid car wreck
doesn't mean I'm going to spare you from
pointing out that being a poet should be more

than a job, more than just mermaids singing
each to each, more than a whine the universe
ignores." So just how well did I know you?

And smiling your lopsided grin, there we
sit in the cafe again, me digging
the pit of my "historical cupidity"

while you demolish everything I say.
The only way that I could tell you were drunk
is how much more logical and fierce

and determinedly fine-grained your arguments
became: it was like watching someone take
a ball-point pen and perform the perfect

tracheotomy, as if the precision
of your violence enabled you to breathe
during The Ten Day War among the bodies:

"Enough bodies," you said, "to know that
anything is possible. I could not
believe what I was seeing. Gunfire in the square

a hundred meters off that I'd only
heard before in partisan movies while I
crouched behind a church wall and translated

for CNN what all these years later
I still refuse to see I saw." And all I can say is,
you were right: we never did swim out

or swim back, we never sat in the sand
and knocked back raki, we never dipped
our fingers into our glasses and rubbed

them on our lips . . . but even so, you can still smell
the grapes and taste the dust they spring from
the same as if you were in the vineyard.

And in every sip, you can taste all the ways
dust tastes—sweet, then bitter, acrid
as gunpowder, a smoky burn to finish.

i.m. Aleš Debeljak

Before Rain

Whatever you do, there are rockets falling,
and after the rockets, smoke climbing

up through walls that are exploding.
Trees grow up where there once were people, weeds

take over beds of lettuces and coddled flowers,
uprearing mole hills unpopulate the fields.

The bricked-in hours of the human have all been knocked down.

No one lingers at lipstick counters, no one
stares into a screen to escape the digital mayhem

of heroes hurdling over the heads of monsters.

The old bones on the mountain that stand upright
and shake when winds blow up from the shore,

old bones that shake when the winds roar

now dangle in the void of an unknown dimension.

Forget all this, says Earth to the stars.

PART TWO

Genie

Who is he, what is he, drifting like a smoke ring as smaller smoke rings drift inside the one just vanishing, always there when the light turns freakish, greenish like tornado light, asking nothing of us, slowly passing through us no matter what we're thinking, feeling, as he expands inside us beyond all measurement, all limit.

There's no god who's more to him than a solitary ant wandering on a countertop.

He declares swamp and desert, the Gowanus Houses across the street, and Louie selling lottery tickets for the Megamillions an outpost the aliens' rocketships will someday reach.

His summer raying out like a crystallized web, he's forever youthful, the erotic anarchist, all moralists disgust him! Old or young, PC or un-PC. Our memories look back at us and see, through him, every wrinkle untransfigured, exactly as we were and are.

Like a worm-hole we pass through each time he looks at us, he brings us face to face with the X-ray/car wreck/the metastasizing future.

In every palm in every lifeline that's shattered, scarred and nicked in its own way, he traces the bastard forms that he most loves and patiently pursues, despite the cops in their cruiser going the wrong way down Wyckoff and the four a.m. gunshots on the corner.

See how, through each of us, he extends his damaged care the way a termite mound extends termite to termite all around the globe.

At the far end of the flea market, where a woman daubs on her customers' wrists her own hand-made perfumes, he brings us to where there are no curtains, to where space outruns the sea like *pi* repeating to infinity in his brain.

As if a split-rail fence, checked and broken all along the grain, were to follow an always shifting dune burying and exposing its own trail as the wind rises, is that how we should follow him? Or does he himself mark off some line of privacy beyond which nobody intrudes?

His heart: never will he leave us totally defenseless, never will he shrug off our sad compulsions.

1

Autobiography

What I was left with was this . . .

—RAYMOND CHANDLER, *FAREWELL, MY LOVELY*

My heart was illiterate, my brain was dangling somewhere
in between. Using the old language of touch and feel,
I took the book and drilled a little hole in the front cover
and strung it up in the poplars in the hot sun.
Half of me was still on the steppes, living the old life
of our first animal-headed gods: deer-headed, lion-headed,
jackal- and bull-headed. The minotaur was the double
of Morgan Johnson's bull alone in the slaughter pens, eyes
tranced on the ground in nearsighted contemplation
of grass blades sharp as steeples rising past hoof-squelch,
piss spatter, muck. Out of my little raw voids
between animal intention and childhood make-believe,
I turned my back to the book and paced off
twenty quick paces, whirled, fired—the pellet
from the gun whirred through the leaves—and I kept on
firing until I found the range so that the book
jerked and leaped at each shot: the pocked
scorched pages spelled a kind of braille
when I ran my fingers over them, fondling
the bumps nippling the paper, a primer
in which I learned that part of us is helpless—
like the man-bull gone wandering in the maze,
too human and too bestial to be borne, a creature that,
despite its rages, its absurd sexual snorts and dainty-toed hooves,
blindly blunders to its eventual slaughter,
ignorant of the butcher-farmer waiting outside
of the double-crossing corridors that twisted in on themselves.
But I'd escape the maze and the liar half god
half man waiting with a concealed weapon inside

the picture book of myths that one summer afternoon
I'd shoot to pieces. And what my freedom gave me
on the far side of the plains were mountains that salt flats
led away from to my promised land of Raymond Chandler,
the total marine darkness between each little beach town
on Highway 101 before the sullen phosphorus
of the cruise ship casino three miles beyond the harbor.
That was when I left the steppes forever, when
the tangled underlife entwined with voices that pricked
and burned, were now flattened to black squiggles on a page
where what comes from the tribe the tribe has lost:
And what I was left with was this: I needed a drink,
I needed a lot of life insurance, I needed a vacation,
I needed a home in the country. What I had was a coat,
a hat and a gun. I put them on and went out of the room.

The Fox

Marine helicopters on maneuver kept dipping
toward swells at Black's Beach, my board's poise
giving way to freefall of my wave tubing

over me, nubs of wax under my feet as I crouched
under the lip, sped across the face and kicked out—
all over Southern Cal a haze settled: as if light breathed

that technicolor smog at sunset over
San Diego Harbor where battleships at anchor,
just back from patrolling the South China Sea, were

having rust scraped off and painted gray.
This was my inheritance that lay stretched before me:
which is when I felt the underbrush give way

and the fox that thrives in my brain,
not looking sly but just at home in his pelt
and subtle paws, broke from cover and ran

across the yard into the future to sniff my gravestone,
piss, and move on. And so I was reborn into
my long nose and ears, my coat's red, white, and brown

giving off my fox smell lying heavy on the winds
in the years when I'd outsmart guns, poison,
dogs and wire, when the rooster and his hens

clucked and ran, crazy with terror
at how everything goes still in that way a fox adores,
gliding through slow-motion drifts of feathers.

Playbook

If you could see the cosmic playbook's *x*'s and *o*'s
all virally mutating, then you'd know as the mind of God knows
that the play would go right, we'd score the touchdown,
but our halfback, gored by three helmets, would rupture his spleen
and die. Despite that, you'd know how much we still
wanted to win, said we were winning in his name,
and though the season was a disaster—we lost all but two games—
his memory was the goalpost we sprinted toward all season.
But at practice, after he died, when we were ramming head-on
into the blocking sled, there'd come a moment of exhaustion
when my mind cleared like a hole in clouds,
and I'd almost stagger and fall to see
that always dying boy's face poking through the blue,
expressing no pain, no recrimination, no fuck you—
just pallid behind the faceguard's shadow cutting
a black line across his nose and eyes like testimony struck
from a report that only the team's collective guilt
could now keep hidden:
                         for that boy, a randy,
square-jawed, loud-mouthed kid played she-male
in the shower room, which led to grab-assing around, boys
squeezing their cocks between their legs, vamping like pinup girls,
as in all that steam we floated beyond bodies
and looked down on ourselves in ritual sanctities
of hooting and pointing and giggling—
                              but something primal
in the bristling pubic hair, as if we'd been touched by a hand
that could change you for real from boy into girl,
made the cheerleaders' pompoms shaking
in your face glisten with a strangeness
that made you blush to see how absurd anatomy
could be, how coerced you were in this body,

mind, this illiterate soul telling the panicked quarterback
to shut up as he moaned, *We need a touchdown*—
and so you, a grunt lineman, slapped his helmet
as if to say, "Call it"—the secret weapon in the playbook:
reverse 4 man 4 hole—
                              and while the quarterback
hyperventilated before shouting out the count,
you knew the reverse was a thing of beauty,
x's stumbling after flying *o*'s as the *o* you were
pulled from the line and cross-body blocked
the linebacker, the crowd's screams ringing inside
your helmet as you rammed him in the gut, knocking
him flat—you owned him, he was bitch, slave—
and you were the heavy dude who always
did his job, clearing the way for the 4 man
to run through the 4 hole and down the sideline
where he'd take the shots for the play
Coach said should only be called once a game.

After the game, after our guy was pronounced dead,
that play sketched out as salvation threaded in reverse
in stop action through your head, frame by frame
jerking him up onto his feet, scissoring legs frozen
forever at the goal line—then again
he runs, again the other team's helmets aimed
at his spine explode from behind to knock
him down, up, down, up running again, his execution
perfect in the playbook's two dimensions until the doc
starts fishing in his black bag and calls the stretcher in.

Net

It was said to be terrible, her temper,
but even more terrible was how she lost it—I mean lost it
in the sense that trees lose leaves,

in that after she lay down on the table
and they gave her electroshock,
her anger simply fell away from her:

it was like watching something or someone musical
go hopelessly, and forever, out of tune.
For the other side of her disease,

the passivity, the compassionating hopelessness
that afflicted her whenever her rage fell away,
now took over—and she saw all too clearly

her exposure high on the cliffs to the hungry beaks
that in her lack of anger, she could no longer
beat back as they swooped down to peck and eat.

Of course none of this happened inside the analytical logics
of my sentences, both too precise and not precise
enough: the flat affect and opacity of her eyes

turned her into a stranger standing just outside the asylum
doorway, staring at children on the lawn on a visiting Sunday
who kept swinging badminton rackets at a birdie,

playing without a net because they'd been told
by other children that the patients weren't allowed
nets because they'd try to steal them

and use them as ladders to escape from their windows
or, worse, try to hang themselves—so she stands there,
and also here, in my sentences that I know didn't know

and still don't know enough about her
to say what her rage, all these years later, might mean.
What do the children know about how hard

it is to play without a net? Do they even notice
how the harder the rackets hit, the higher and more gracefully
the birdie floats until it soars above the net

that isn't there and, up among the trees, gets lost in falling leaves?

———————

When she calls me today, only minutes ago,
to tell me the unalloyed stuff
of her dream, she's riding on what she calls

"that hot-bottomed bus, when we were
all coming home, and there were chickens
flying around the bus, and a little pig

in a wooden cage in the aisle,
and when we stopped I said to a man,
Where are we? and he said in perfect English,

In Mexico, and there were a lot of tourist shops," she said,
"and so I got off the bus to look, and there was a balloon man
selling helium balloons," and she said, "Oh Tom,

the balloons were all so colorful,
and there was one of a cow, a bright yellow cow,
and I wanted that one so badly, such a beautiful cow,

and when I looked around, the bus was gone
and I was left alone but there were
hundreds of yellow cows all floating above the street."

That Word

i.m. Philip Levine

He sits reading under his desk lamp,
he loves how wind distresses tail and mane,
he likes the rhymes internal and irregular,
how people from the old days walk in and out
of the poem, how the father who dies
in one stanza can rise in another, how, despite
the drought, the rain keeps falling in fourteen lines.
His rumpled bed is never not specific
as the dent his head leaves in the pillow.
He rubs his hand across his jaw, unshaven,
his touch on the back of your wrist is delicate
and urgent, when you help him up from bed,
he isn't shy about holding on, when he lies
back down, he grips his water bottle and won't
let go. Smiling, says: Let's not use that word:
it's been used ten thousand eight-hundred
and seventy-six times. He shrugs off the weepers,
the brotherly lovers, the sour preachers turning
purple and blue in their dandruff-sprinkled robes.
Out in his backyard in Fresno, the oranges are ripening.
At his window in Brooklyn, the plane trees,
stripped bare of leaves, click softly in the breeze.
Him in his undershirt, in his tweed jacket,
in sweat pants watching Norbert Schemansky clean and jerk.
Now he's throwing rocks on the bridle path,
he's turning into a fox, the brush of his tail
mocks the pack, he leaps clear of his own tracks,
doubles back, loses the lords and ladies riding.
Now he's preaching to rats, showing them pages
in Holy Books, Money Books, Books of the Entitled
that are good to eat and chew right down.

But all alone in his study with ice and sun, he scrawls
with his fountain pen, crosses it all out, starts again:
and this time rising up are the sheared away walls
of an abandoned highschool, a stack of rusted axles,
a diner where nobody talks openly
of love but where ketchup and mockery
are served up with the coffee and his heart,
arrhythmic, pulses out of synch, all on its own.

What the Dog Really Says

It wasn't language but "eyeage" the dog spoke,
looking at the door, then at me, then at the door—
its eyes signaling something more than what Chekhov
said the dog smelled in each corner of the room—
the unquestioned superiority of human beings.
Nor was it what Nietzsche thought, when he wrote
that a dog comes up to the philosopher as if to ask a question,
but then forgets the question—for there was no question
when the dog licked the hand, there was a smell of a kind
that the dog must have known so well from when the hand
took it out for walks and the dog plunged its nose
into frozen meat of a gull on a day so cold
only the faintest microbial whiffs of rot could thread their way
up the dog's nostrils and knot and unknot in its brain.
What the dog really says is that if a dog could talk,
we couldn't understand it. And so the dog moves
in harmony of nose to smell, claws clicking
on the sidewalk as it marks with a squirt this tree,
that fence post, the laminar overlays of scent like pages
leafed through in a diary in which each entry keeps changing
in a present that has no future but only a fading past.
For three days and nights, the dog didn't move
from under the bed where the man whose hand
it licked for the salts on the hand, the subtly changing salts,
lay unmoving. But why did the dog keep lying there
once the body was zipped away into a body bag,
wrestled onto a gurney as the undertaker, unshaven,
in rumpled white shirt with maybe gravy stains on the collar,
his black slacks and jacket fitting a little too tight, tried to make
the dog move until the dog showed its teeth and began to bark?
What's in the dog-hearted dog-brained dog's heart?

And why would we say that a dog is afraid his master will beat
    him today
but not that a dog is afraid his master will beat him tomorrow?
The salts on the man's hand, did they smell and taste of what a dog
smells and tastes when it rolls on its back in half-rotten flesh,
and comes running with that odor wafting from its matted down fur
toward the hand that feeds it and that it licks?
Things to be eaten, smelled, sat upon, run away from,
things that die but don't make a dog fearful,
the many ways dogs bark in the dwindling languages
bow-wow blaf-blaf hau-hau gong-gong tyav-tyav—
what does the dog know of this, its features scrunching up
into a puggish, wrinkled I'm-worried-shouldn't-you-be face?

Face

i.m. Mark Strand

Mark came into the room and said, *Tom, you have
the face of a dog. Alan, you have the face
of a horse. And me, I have the face of—*

but Mark couldn't decide what kind of face
he had, or else I couldn't in the dream
remember or maybe it was that the dream

couldn't remember. And in the second part
of the dream Mark came into the room smiling
and laughing, and after a while he left the room

and Alan said, *It's only natural he wants
to have a good time.* And when Mark didn't come
back for a while, I went looking for him,

and though I knew where he was, I couldn't find him.
And in the third part of the dream, Mark came
back into the room and said, *No, Alan, you*

*have the face of a dog, Tom, you have
the face of a horse, and me, I have—*
but he never did say what kind of face he had.

And in the fourth part of the dream, Mark came
back into the room and said, *No, no, it's me!
I have the face of a horse! I have the face of a dog!*

And in the fifth part of the dream—
but there was no fifth part of the dream—
only Alan, me, horse, dog, and Mark

coming and going, coming and going in the room.

Dragon

The dragon huddling in its coils won't come out. It lies dreaming in its scales, as forgotten as an old vacuum cleaner in a broom closet. Despite the stink of cordite and sulfur on its breath, how it hated, in its youth, the no quarter duels against those berserk Anglo-Saxon sons of Wulf, and later, the tin cans on horseback calling themselves knights. At least their horses, who hated fire, had enough sense to be afraid. So much repetition in a life, so much wasted time, so much courtly blather. The dragon wants no more of it, no more vomiting fire on a town of orange trees near the Atlas Mountains, so that a YouTube video can show the liberators celebrating what to the dragon is so boring he's yawning before the first hair on the enemy's head is singed (these monotheists, as every dragon knows, are the worst). To the dragon, the broom closet, dusty, dark, smelling of shoe polish and bleach, broomstraw tickling its nose, is as close to freedom, to feeling unmixed happiness, as the dragon has ever known. And such dreams the dragon dreams, mother dreams and father dreams, tempters and orgies, and one special dream of a girl dragon who keeps changing into a boy! Such joy to be shut away from the octaves above high C, the meat slab faces of heroes warbling and braying *basso profundo*, just begging to be barbecued in their armor. And as for the one who would knock his wine glass on the floor, and go looking for the broom, reaching his hand into the dark, does he risk having his flesh scorched to the very bone? Or does the dragon, so forgetful of itself that it flinches at the lightest touch, spread its wings and fly away?

For Brigit Kelly

The void draws a magic
circle around her arms, legs, and head
dissolving into the flashing hieroglyphic
that reigns over the dead.

Like a bird-footed stylus a song incises
itself in drying clay. All that's left by
midnight once her singing ceases
is a burned-over field knowing nothing of her sky

or how a thousand years on some spiral
of her song's DNA will still be epic.
Meanwhile, in the shadows a scorpion's tail

arches high over its back,
daring, fearful,
keeping watch over her soul's vulnerable republic.

2

House of Fact, House of Ruin

1 / HOMILIES FROM HOME

You've got to put your pants on in the house of fact.
And in the house of fact, when you take off your shirt,
you can hear your shirt cry out, *Facts are the floor, facts*
are how you make the right side talk to the left.

I'm washing my naked belly clean, and doing it with dignity.
I'm turning around, trying to see the filthiness
that keeps making me filthy. I've scraped away
my molecules right down to the atoms' emptiness

and arranged the map's folds so that nobody
can see it breaking into fits of weeping.
Now that even our eyes have their dedicated poverties,

now that even our eyes are chained to their slavish occupations,
whatever the soul lacks drains the soul to nothing.
I hate to admit it, but even the house of fact is a house of ruin.

2 / REST

The strange is done with, over,
the strange that late at night you returned
to chat with again and again. No longer will anyone
wait for me in my corner where

good is bad, where that tight-lipped morning
of tears by the bay means nothing anymore
to anyone. To be cleared of the inks that stain
my ankles while watching my eyes go blind in the mirror

is the kind of rest that the seventh day promises
but never brings. Instead, the species
climbs aboard the ark of copulation

and ignores the forty days and nights of rain.
And the much talked of soul that the rain denies
burrows deep into the mud of so much pain.

3 / SPIDER

Look at the spider with the enormous body and tiny head,
a spider of no color: today, when I kneel
down to look at it more closely, its many arms nailed
to a many-armed cross are a prayer in a code that only God,

who's forgotten it, can decipher. And its eyes
invisible to my eyes, which guided it like a pilot
through the wilderness of space,
no longer steer its legs across the intricate,

almost-not-thereness of its web. Each thread
it spins with the finality of fate divides its head
from its body. And the poor thing,

even with so many legs, doesn't know which way to run.
Just look at its abdomen, huge as the stone blocking
what's-his-name's tomb, that the head's condemned to drag around.

4 / IF THE SUN SHOULD BLACKEN TO AN ASTERISK

Honestly, when I look at life straight,
I'm just another blind Brooklynite—not because
I can't see that Jean-Jacques was an idiot,
or that Saint Peter being nailed to the cross

upside down isn't the purest measure
of my humanity, but because my eyes
can't see my illiterate skeleton, and the razor
and cigar that will outlive me. So try to save a day

for when there are no days, reason with the lens
inside every healing wound, witness how your
own inner grace, gnawing at itself, gets baptized
in phosphates of hemlock and error.

And so what if the sunset arrives from Athens?
So what if no trace of anyone survives?

5 / THE LAST TO BE EXCUSED

Remember the old aunts, sarcastic,
chainsmoking, gesturing with their canes,
scoring point after point with their widowed lungs?

How was I to eat with them as they pushed
around their plates not peas and carrots
but distance and disdain for their silly nephew

still trying, at his age, to forget
how being old is as new to the old
as being just born is to the just born—

even their glued-together, half-cracked
china radiates impatience for the pity
that the young want them to want.

The way they kept saying MOTHER—
like it was all in caps—saying it like that
as if they still felt her eyes on how

they handled their knives, forks, spoons,
making each bite harder to swallow.
The day is coming when there'll be no water

in the pitcher, no eternally dying father
served up like canned spinach and corn,
no brooches of affection their absent lips

pin to the air. And as that silence
slowly breaks the hours in two, I'll be
left alone to dine with the nothingness

that, just for form's sake, says grace.
The table will be set with shadows,
the phantom food served up by shadows—

and all the dead mothers come to this repast
will sit down on chairs of dust
in the wake of that last supper

in the kitchen gone cold where I'll hear the last
maternal "Serve yourself, Tom"
smothered by that dark where no one can tell

the knife blade from the handle,
or the food from the plate, or the plate
from the table, or if there's a table at all.

6 / THE ETERNAL DICE

OMG, it makes me cry to admit that I am human;
to feel the heaviness of all your bread I've eaten.

Oh sure, you claimed you raised me from the dust,
but where's the wound fermenting in your side?

You know nothing of those Marias who split for good.
OMG, if you'd been born a human being

today you'd know how to behave like God.
But in your always everywhere hard partying with perfection

you feel nothing of the pain of your creation.
And so it's us, the poor fuckers who suffer, who must be god.

Today, in my middle-aged pupils, I see the glare of candles
lit for my death-row vigil. OMG, old gambler, take up

your crooked tricks again, and let's throw your cooked pair of dice—
in the fated luck you dole out to the universe

maybe we'll roll snake eyes staring back at us like death,
maybe you'll deal two aces black as the grave's mud.

OMG, in this night gone deaf and blind,
you won't be able to play because the poor Earth itself

is just a single die whose edges have grown rounded
by rolling too many eons through the battering sky

and nobody now can stop it until it rolls into a hole,
the vast hole, OMG, inside a single molecule.

7 / THE OTHER GARDEN

In the Garden there was a spider.
And because the man knelt beside him, the spider
overheard him, the agony of his prayer
like the fear of a fly who can't steer

any other direction than into the web stretching out
no matter which way the fly veers. The spider
felt the threads of all being vibrate
through him—and so it vowed to be the answer

to the prayer of the man praying to his father
to let this cup pass. But on the cross, when the man cried out
to his father not to abandon him, his father

did abandon him. And so the spider
vowed to weave a web so tightly around the father
that the harder he'd struggle the more he'd be caught.

8 / WHAT HASN'T YET COME IS ALREADY OVER

If it rains tonight, will a raindrop be my cell?
Will the bars the sky lets down
take one look at me and turn to steel?
Now that the hot afternoon is finally done,

done the cups of tea we drank with your mother,
I want to ask the rain to yank my strings
back a thousand years. But even back that far,
will the rain still be my prison?

To be lost in the minutiae
of our vacations from the soul, to forget
the vedic threads spun out beyond my end,

to press against your breasts obedient
to the purest pulses. Yeah, sure. Make the story
of my life the story of my never having been.

3

At the Harbor Lounge

A harpoon above glass sliders in the noisy bar,
olives in a martini glass shining an unearthly green,
the vodka, as I sip it, tastes good, tastes bitter,
tastes a little salty, almost bloody, the way
my tongue tastes when I bite it. The guy on
the banquette across from me is making out,
he has his hand down the back of the other guy's jeans,
but it's leisurely, familiar, the six month
half-life of finally getting to know
somebody's mouth. The swords and flames
tattooed on his bicep thrust and ripple,
as if another body lived inside his body
and was showing me, me alone, its plan
to break free and live, forever, the good life.
Now a rain squall over the waves twitches, twists,
anxiety shows me to myself in the older guys'
wrinkles, I watch my gargoyle face wrap around
the belly of my cocktail glass. Is it just booze
talking or do I really, really and truly,
not recognize that nose, those eyes?
Desire holding itself back to give itself later,
everybody with their buttons waiting
to be pushed, sadness inside pleasure inside
whatever prison the body inside
my body wants release from. Two drinks down,
and it's like somebody's shooting a movie
of my life in two inch close-ups so all
you can see is the moonscape of my pores.

Adventure

The little piano sonata that has that little lift
at the end of each phrase penetrates
the late-night discussion of how manboobs
and marriage and gay and straight don't begin
to make clear what the notes, "fine and tragic,"
fallible and consoling, keep telling the air
about how bodies disappear. Above our heads,
up through the ceiling, we can hear now and then
what sounds like people fucking though we know
it's just something, a tree limb, maybe,
being battered by the wind in that rising rhythm
of a man who wrote that "after years of
vaporizing and poetic screaming, I had
managed to make one of my poems smile."
But that smile, he says, was an adventure
that "ended with my practical acceptance
and understanding of male loneliness . . ."
When I was a kid, I remember banging
out notes and pressing the hold pedal
so that overtones vibrating through my body
made me all weepy, out of sheer confusion
in all that Romantic boom and quaver.
I never told anyone about this, and afterward,
I wouldn't, out of some fear I still don't wholly
understand, touch the keyboard . . . refusing
to lose myself in the spaces between notes
becoming ever more quiet, constantly
branching out into ever thinner air.

Dead Gull

Waking at four, waking again at six,
there it is again, splayed out in its own halo
of feathers blowing whitely in the wind,
the other gulls standing around it, looking
sleepy or stupefied by sun and cold, oblivious
to its lumpen heaviness, its casual *I-don't-care.*
They flew away when I came closer and bent down—
intestines, torn from the belly, lay a foot
from the body, looping and coiling, so brilliant,
so red, infested by sandfleas ricocheting
off my shoes. "Bad for me, good for you," said
the woman last night in the bar, pushing
her girlfriend out the door, who kept yelling,
"I'm happy, I'm happy!—what's wrong with that?"
I beat my absurd little wings beating
them so fast to lift me one inch off the ground,
I fly a little ways—a little farther—crash,
hobble, drag and flap my feathers, nestle
in the dune, eyes shutting, beak useless against
this weakness, waves crashing far off coming
closer—waking at eight for good, my body
is foxed glass rattling in its frame—then caffeine,
the shower streaming over me, the usual
anxiety when the razor scrapes my face.
Through the sea's lens I see myself dwindling
to this open clamshell rawness sluicing
the fine grit the tides pour through me,
letting some things go, trapping others.

Kangaroo

Lights grapple naked in the puddles.
From one end of the street to the other,
nothing's moving but the rain. Bodies shifting
in the waiting room, women with big purses
and wearing lots of lipstick, the man
next to me jangling the bangles on his arms,
their shadows scale the TV light up across
the wall. You float among the Forms
in your hospital bed, lips painted blue.
Is your coma just part of your extravagance?
When I was just born, they put me
in the incubator's plastic pouch of oxygen—
each time you asked to see me, they brought you
my twin brother—but you knew it wasn't me:
and when they finally showed me to you,
you said I was tiny, like that baby kangaroo
in the video you love: together
we'd watch it, blind, furless, no bigger
than my thumb, climb from the womb up
the mountain of the mother's belly to slip
into her pouch and suckle on a nipple—
but only the fittest survive that journey.
I want to think we'll meet again as animals,
wordless in the pouch's lick and nuzzle.
But when the strangers came and asked
in their strange tongue that odd beast's name,
an indigenous man said, "Kangaroo, kangaroo"—
meaning, *I don't understand you.*

Little Myth

for my father

I wipe the dust off your picture, polish
your reading glasses and put them on:
you stare at me with such frank simplicity
it reminds me of that pair
of old black jeans with the paint stains,
the ones I've saved at the back of my closet,
thinking one day I'd try them on—
the only pair of jeans you ever owned—
but no, they're not yours, though I like
to pretend they are—my little myth
made up to keep you near . . .
The dark behind you in the photo
pushes your face so far beyond the frame I can
feel your bony body hugging mine:
white-skinned legs, sparsely haired shanks,
calves slender but hard-muscled,
hipbone with the metal pin in it.
Half your face in shadow, half bright lit,
your eyes signal your skeptic need
to love so as not to be hurt
by being loved. For you, did love
mean all that you could do
by loving others, your sacrifice
of disappearing into their eyes?
Your death that's never over keeps
shifting what I feel. In the blackness
of the background your stare gives form to
your love for me keeps our distance near.

Party

I'm hauling young Tom and old dying Tom
out of the crevasse hand over hand, until yes,
I can see them through dark and mist,
they're calling my name, *Tom, Tom,*
and as I lift them free of clouds into the center
of a clearing in the air lit by molten ice—
I see old Tom has scars on his face
from young Tom's cuts still bleeding—
and then the rope burns through
my hands, I can't hold either
one, I'm weak, I'm dying—and now
the three of us plunge so far down I can't tell
if we're moving as we're falling
suspended in the no time of the fall.
Now I see faces at a party, and under
the faces more faces, and bodies
afloat in cocktail hour light,
and this woman whose perfect skin
fits her so poorly it won't stop
writhing around under her clothes.
And in another room it's like I've come
to your room where we're lying there naked,
our humps and bumps of undisguised flesh
indistinguishably so other and alienly
ourselves that sex tears me away into
another room—a small room containing
itself but not knowing what's inside it
in its full emptiness emptying itself out.

Prayer

When my happiness goes unmuted, if happiness
it is, I can drive you crazy with my need to talk,
my babbling anti-eloquence that won't let up
showing every moment the threadbareness
of my being, how my mind, misfiring,
frictioning into smoke, administers
a shock—or if my mood shifts and I try
to back off, but the day keeps asking
unanswerable questions, I want to be
no more than the absence under
a sofa cushion, hidden from your eyes
that I'm afraid will both pity and despise me
or worse, love me, seeing through
my need to be both pitied and despised.
And so my shame in front of you makes
me watch myself turn into a fly hugging
plate glass, my nine hearts beating
in such excess of emotion I feel myself
quiver, feet slippering up the pane
in an anxious, aimless dance, wings
battering forward going nowhere
but whirling so fast they disappear—as if
God, or a god, held me suspended here,
a specimen before your eyes that can't see
in me any trace of human anymore—now turning
your back on me, as if setting me free to be
just another mote of transparency I
shimmer through swerving away in sunlit air.

Funeral Oration

When I think of myself dead, there I am
joking around at my own funeral, white-faced death
putting his mask on my face, and even though
I'm dead, I'm hoping whoever's standing there
will think my jokes are funny, an antidote to
having had to push me in a rented wheelchair
or worry about my white count,
or witness my living will. There we'll
be, my twin brother Tim and me, Tim with
a trowel trying to dig a little hole
to put a baggie full of ashes in, maybe a little
annoyed in his love of me for still telling jokes,
wanting him to laugh, though let's face it,
my timing, like now, always sucked.
And other of my faults, my taking things too personally,
or my certainty that I knew the world better
than my brother did, or my know-it-all
attitudes about raising kids, or my silly
conviction that tidiness was a balm to the soul,
all that comes back to everyone I loved
and whispers in their ears, *God yes,*
he could be a trial, a pain to himself, to us—
anyway, may none of this warp or maim
anyone's heart—and not too many tears,
Sarah and Hannah, not too many tears before
you go off to your separate lives again, not
too much sadness when you stand by the stove
talking so long the tea gets cold before you sip it.

Long Distance

Like a cartoon skeleton I see myself in my coffin
talking on a cellphone to your skeleton
in your coffin, whispering, *So what are you wearing?*
Is this what our love requires—to be embarrassed
but not embarrassed by how unlovely
or needy or gauche our bodies are?
Whenever you're away, I worry more than ever
that you'll die before I die, reminded by
the scars when your nightgown caught on fire
to hold you even closer, to not feel ashamed
or apologetic but weirdly grateful each time
I touch that damage making me more tender,
less scared of being yours. And yet the touching
itself doesn't care, doesn't know who we are—
as if flesh were just the catalyst vanishing
into the flame-up of a chemical reaction
in which pleasure takes us over,
so all we do is hover above what touch
is doing to us, our nakedness
so neutral as if we were mapped on Google,
but coming down to street level
we're bewildered to find it's us.
If only touch didn't need your body
and my body to be touched, then the one who dies
first could really wait for the other,
could follow the other's scars
and climb back into this world where our flesh
would still burn, still scar, and still be ours.

Hannah Reading Hemingway

To have that feel for things Nick has down
in the depths of your nineteen years
out fishing your own big two-hearted river
where hoppers on Nick's hook tense their legs against
the strike, wings whirring as they drown,
are you learning to hold steady against the cold current
near the bottom?—saying, as you turn my copy's yellowed
pages, how you love Nick for his loneliness,
his isolation the words make yours in your tenderness
for him. And when I read how the old waiter prays,
Our nada who art in nada, nada be thy name,
and think how some form of his despair
might one day be your despair, I see no clean,
well-lighted place hovering in your future:
but my mad Tom world, which may seem quaintly
reassuring to what really might be coming,
seems like so much posturing when I look at your selfies—
your beautifully stubbled, shaved head on one side
while the other side grows long and tangled
like your mother's. In your need for people,
in our need for you, in this world where
there's no waiter, no Nick, only this *nada*
that your mother and I are fast becoming,
what will outlast our disappearing?
As if we were old trout all badged with sores
Nick reaches your hand down underwater
to where we lie stunned on the stones, and your finger
gently wakes us, nudging us back swerving down the river.

Island

Above the sea how useless this mist is, as useless
as the sea, as useless as a birthday over sixty.
All the men and women happy to be their age,
do they ever feel my old guy's solace
in self-estrangement, my relief in suddenly
feeling room on room swept clean of me?
How much of what sustained me as a kid
survives? I feel almost bodiless, the surge before
a quarrel no more than a skeleton's bluster,
dull cousin to all the bones rattling the world.
Thickening around the lone sailboat still at anchor
from the summer, mist erases the slender mast,
rubs out the small black ducks like flaws on paper
where whatever is written writes itself invisibly.
—So still this morning. Mist thickens, wanes, no breeze
rattles the dead hydrangeas or leaves
its fingerprints on the water. No arms
and bodies flash above the sea dissolved
in mist all the way to the vanishing jetty.
Such an arbitrary number, sixty—
not an anchoring place, nothing to give
resistance to the ripples spreading, dying away.
Yet why, between the wreck sunk just beyond
the harbor, and all the ways on shore that harm
comes cruising out of nowhere, do I
feel such stasis, such almost peace to find
myself here, as if just this moment I
were an island the sea is sinking from.

Notes

General Note

Many of these poems use as a springboard a trip to Libya I took in the spring of 2014, just as the country was entering its second civil war.

Lizards

Erwin Rommel, the famed German WWII tank commander during the North African campaign in Libya, was christened the Desert Fox by British journalists.

The first image of the lizard is taken from Adam Nicolson's *Why Homer Matters*, and the final image is taken from Antoine de Saint-Exupéry.

For a Libyan Militia Member

In Libya in 2014, I traveled with a Libyan militia for a week. This poem is based on a young militia member who had suffered shrapnel wounds to his face during the Revolution.

A Drone in the Promised Land

I visited the town of Quneitra, Syria, in 2007. Seized by Israel during the 1968 Six Day War, the Israeli forces withdrew from the town in 1974 after the Yom Kippur War. The buildings were stripped right down to the doorknobs, and anything that was salvageable was sold off to Israeli contractors. The town when I visited was a ruin, as well as doubling as a Syrian propaganda site.

The speaker of this poem is alternately a human being and a drone. Or perhaps both at the same time.

Propaganda

The poem is based on an interview with Bouthaina Shaaban, the Syrian Minister of Expatriates, in 2007.

The Advance

"Zubrak" is an Arabic vulgarism for penis.

Lady Justice

The poem is dedicated to the memory of James Foley, a freelance journalist who was beheaded by the Islamic State militant, "Jihadi John" (Mohammed Emwazi).

Enhanced Interrogation Techniques

The poem draws on several interviews with Tony Lagouranis.

The second sonnet is a rewriting of Robert Frost's "Silken Tent."

Where the Magic Ends

The poem takes off from "Ali Baba and the Forty Thieves" in *One Thousand and One Nights*.

Al-Mutanabbi Street is the famous bookseller's street in Baghdad that has been the heart of the book trade and a literary center since the 8th century. It was named after one of the Arab world's most famous poets, Abu al-Tayyib Ibn al-Husayn al-Mutanabbi.

Kibera

A vast shanty town in the middle of Nairobi, and the largest in Africa. Kibera has been estimated to number anywhere between 170,000 in 2009 to over 1,000,000 people today, depending on the boundaries and the census methods employed.

The ending of the poem paraphrases some observations in Pliny the Elder's *Historia Naturalis (Natural History)*.

What Is

The poem mentions several paintings by Piero della Francesca as well as a painting by Fredric Church.

Negatives

The quotes are taken from Walt Whitman's *Specimen Days*.

The Drowned and the Saved

In *If This Is a Man* (in English known as *Survival in Auschwitz*), Primo Levi quotes Dante's Canto 26, about the drowning of Ulysses, to a fellow camp inmate.

Down from the Mount

The poem is based on the incidents at Le Bataclan, the nightclub in Paris where ninety people were killed by Islamic militants in 2015.

The poem also draws on Plato's *Phaedrus* and the *Odyssey*.

All the Ways Dust Tastes

The poem is dedicated to the memory of the Slovenian poet, Aleš Debeljak.

That Word

Philip Levine had a lifelong heart arrhythmia. The word is "love."

What the Dog Really Says

The poem borrows "eyeage" from an essay on animal language by Samuel Butler.

Dragon

I have always wondered what a dragon would think of Wagner, and his dragon-slaying Siegfried.

For Brigit Kelly

The poem takes its image of the scorpion from her poem "Iskandariya."

Adventure

The quote is from the diaries of Cesare Pavese.

Hannah Reading Hemingway

The prayer is from Ernest Hemingway's short story "A Clean, Well-Lighted Place."

Acknowledgments

The American Poetry Review: "What Is"

The Atlantic: "Down from the Mount" (under the title, "Cricket")

The Berlin Journal: "Kibera"

Birmingham Poetry Review: "My Tiger" and "Playbook"

Consequence: "List," "Dream," "Litany," "Negatives," and "All the Ways Dust Tastes"

Great River Review: "Autobiography"

Hunger Mountain: "Enhanced Interrogation Techniques" and "Lady Justice"

The New Yorker: "The Fox"

Plume: "The Drowned and the Saved" and "Genie"

Poetry: "The Advance" and "House of Fact, House of Ruin"

Raritan: "A Drone in the Promised Land" and "For a Libyan Militia Member"

The Southern Review: "Propaganda"

The Threepenny Review: "Net" and "That Word" (under the title, "For Phil")

Tikkun: "Before Rain"

The text of *House of Fact, House of Ruin* is set in Adobe Garamond Pro. Book design by Rachel Holscher. Composition by Bookmobile Design and Digital Publisher Services, Minneapolis, Minnesota. Manufactured by [TK] on acid-free, [TK] percent postconsumer wastepaper.

TOM SLEIGH's many books of poetry include *Station Zed*, *Army Cats*, winner of the John Updike Award from the American Academy of Arts and Letters, and *Space Walk*, which received the Kingsley Tufts Poetry Award. In addition, *Far Side of the Earth* won an Academy Award from the American Academy of Arts and Letters, *The Dreamhouse* was a finalist for the *Los Angeles Times* Book Prize, and *The Chain* was a finalist for the Lenore Marshall Poetry Prize. Sleigh is also the author of two books of essays, *The Land between Two Rivers: Writing in an Age of Refugees* and *Interview with a Ghost*. He has received the Poetry Society of America's Shelley Prize, and fellowships from the Guggenheim Foundation, two from the National Endowment for the Arts, and many other awards. His work appears in the *New Yorker*, *Poetry*, as well as in *The Best of the Best American Poetry*, *The Best American Travel Writing*, and *The Pushcart Anthology*. He is a Distinguished Professor at Hunter College and has worked as a journalist in the Middle East and Africa. Sleigh lives in New York.